M000106808

This book is dedicated to my stepfamily....

Jim, Jon and Michael, my children by birth

Karen, Julie and Bill, my children by marriage

Roger, their father and my husband....whose patience and caring brought us together.

WOODLAND PRESS
99 WOODLAND CIRCLE
MINNEAPOLIS, MN 55424
(612) 926-2665

PRINTED IN THE U.S.A.

ADDITIONAL COPIES: For individual
copies send $6.95 plus applicable tax and
$2.50 to cover the cost of handling to
WOODLAND PRESS.
QUALITY DISCOUNT RATES are
available for hospitals, schools, churches
and others who need more than 12 copies.
write for details

ABOUT THIS BOOK

This book was created to help children learn about stepfamilies. It will inform, prepare and guide both children and adults during a confusing time. It will help children work through natural feelings resulting from family change and help parents identify problems and children's individual needs.

Because of unresolved grief and loyalty conflicts, children often do not share a parent's joy and enthusiasm when they marry again. Children who are unable to understand or verbally express negative or ambivalent feelings often act them out in negative ways. The art process allows children to express their ideas, feelings and perceptions about self and others symbolically. Conflict can be resolved, self esteem increased and coping skills developed.

The educational concepts are presented in six units and should be followed in order. Each child will need a small box of crayons. Crayons are suggested because they are more effective for expressing feelings than markers. Ask children to draw any picture that comes into their mind when they read each page. They may ask for more directions or suggestions but need to be encouraged to make their own decisions and draw their own thoughts. Emphasize ideas and expressions rather than drawing ability. Older children may prefer colored pencils and include more words. When thinking about difficult emotional issues children often regress and scribble, erase, cross-out or draw something unrelated.

It is important to have a supportive adult available to acknowledge and accept the child's feelings and encourage communication. Books from the adult reading list should be read before beginning. Supplemental reading for children is also suggested.

SUGGESTED READING FOR CHILDREN

Berman, Claire. WHAT AM I DOING IN A STEPFAMILY?, N.Y., N.Y.: Carol Publishing, 1992

Boyd, Lizi. THE NOT-SO-WICKED STEPMOTHER, N.Y., N.Y. Puffin Books, 1987

Boyd, Lizi. SAM IS MY HALF BROTHER, N.Y., N.Y. Puffin Books, 1990

Coleman, Wm. WHAT YOU SHOULD KNOW ABOUT GETTING ALONG WITH A NEW PARENT,
        Mpls: Augsburg, 1992

Drescher, Joan. MY MOTHER'S GETTING MARRIED, N.Y., N.Y. Pied Piper, 1989

Phillips, Carolyn. OUR FAMILY GOT A STEPPARENT, Ventura, CA: Regal Books, 1981

Supe, Gretchen. WHAT KIND OF FAMILY DO YOU HAVE?, N.Y.: Twenty-First Century Books, 1991

SUGGESTED READING FOR ADULTS

Burns, Cherie. STEPMOTHERHOOD, First Perennial Lib. ED. N.Y.: Perennial Library, 1986

Kaplan, Leslie. COPING WITH STEPFAMILIES, N.Y.: Rosen Publishing, 1986

Mala, Burt. STEPFAMILIES STEPPING AHEAD, Lincoln, NE: Stepfamily Assoc. of America, 1989

Prilik, Pearl. STEPMOTHERING - ANOTHER KIND OF LOVE, N.Y.: Berkley, 1990

Savage, K. & Adams, P. THE GOOD STEPMOTHER, N.Y.: Crowne Pub., 1988

Wallerstein, Judith & Kelly, Joan. SURVIVING THE BREAK UP, N.Y.: Basic Books, 1980

SUGGESTED READING FOR PROFESSIONALS

Hodges, Wm. INTERVENTIONS FOR CHILDREN OF DIVORCE, N.Y.: Wiley, 1986

Martin, Don & Maggie. STEPFAMILIES IN THERAPY, San Francisco: Jossey-Bass, 1992

Visher, Emily & John. SAME OLD LOYALTIES, NEWS TIES: Therapeutic Strategies With Stepfamilies
        N.Y.: Brunner/Mazel, 1988

FOR ADDITIONAL SUGGESTIONS

Contact: Stepfamily Association of America Inc.
                215 Centennial Mall South, Lincoln, NE 68508 - 1834   (402) 477-STEP

TO PARENTS:

Before stepfamilies come together, first families come apart . . . usually by death or divorce. Family loss and change brings confusion, conflict and grief. Adult joys of remarriage may not be shared by children who often feel abandoned and wonder if they are still loved. Remarriage often changes a close child/parent relationship bringing new losses including the fantasy that the family will be reunited. Special times, roles and responsibilities in the family change. Death and divorce can shatter a child's trust in relationships. They need to recognize and express feelings in order to accept their losses and feel free to love others.

Stepparents are often unwanted relationships and many try too hard to be accepted. Children and stepparents don't have to love each other! Instant love is unrealistic. It takes time and patience to earn trust and respect. A child's mourning process may not be completed until they become an adult and leave home. Some memories need to be grieved and resolved to be released and others need to be kept as cherished links to a personal past.

Storybook myths of the wicked stepmother complicate a new role for women and confusion regarding legal responsibility and money issues challenge both spouses. Children need adult influence and discipline but they resent anyone trying to take a birth parent's place. Unfortunately, the stepparent most needed is the one often rejected.

Resentments flourish from demands to share time, money and energy. Children's feelings are magnified in the search for identity and security with extra rivalry and competition. Recognize that a child's difficult behavior is often a struggle to put his/her life back together and not a personal attack. It is as important to reward good behavior as it is to be consistent with punishment. All children must be treated fairly and recognized as individuals with different interests, abilities and needs.

Boundaries must be flexible to allow space to make mistakes to learn and grow. Family meetings involving the entire family can be a time to discuss problems and create specific house rules and disciplinary practices. Counseling for support with difficult issues and help in defining problems and goals can be helpful.

This mourning and resentment takes place when the couple wants to experience joy and is trying to build a new relationship. Spouses must support each other in front of children. They need to take time to develop a strong interpersonal relationship and should plan weekly dinners for two and regular weekends together in order to direct their energies to what can be changed and accept that which cannot be changed. They need to develop and nurture a sense of humor and the ability to laugh at some everyday difficulties.

This book was developed to teach children concepts about stepfamilies and to help them develop skills for coping with family change. Drawing encourages verbal communication and reveals children's concerns and misconceptions. The following objectives are included in the text and may be stressed by additional reading from suggested books.

I. CHANGE IS A PART OF LIFE   p.1-5

    Recognize change as a part of life
    Identify ways of coping with change
    Recognize family changes
    Discuss personal changes

II. UNDERSTANDING STEPFAMILIES p.6-10

    Identify misconceptions
    Assess unreaslistic expectations
    Learn healthy concepts of stepfamilies
    Encourage acceptance of new family

III. RECOGNIZING FEELINGS   p.11-15

    Learn about the grief process
    Recognize/name feelings
    Accept all feelings as O.K.
    Identify personal feelings

IV. EXPRESSING FEELINGS   p. 16-21

    Identify fears and worries
    Learn healthy ways to express feelings
    Recognize personal problems
    Share difficult feelings and concerns

V. FEELING O.K. ABOUT ME   p.22-27

    Learn to communicate concerns
    Identify support systems
    Discuss guilt feelings
    Increase confidence and self esteem

VI. LIVING IN A STEPFAMILY p.28-32

    Recognize individual stengths
    Stengthen relationships
    Develop self care skills
    Encourage positive expectations

FOR CHILDREN:

This book was written to help you understand the many feelings children have when a parent marries again. It is a happy time for your parent but it can be a confusing time for you because of the many changes in your life. This book will help you and your family understand each other better.

This is your book! You will make it special as you draw the picture that comes into your mind as you read the words on each page. There will never be another book like yours because everyone has different thoughts and feelings.

You do not have to be able to draw or color well to add your thoughts and feelings to this book. You will just need a small box of crayons to draw lines, shapes and perhaps a few words to tell some things you think or feel about the changes in your life. There is no right or wrong way. Do it your way. It is your book.

Begin with the first page and do the pages in order. When you have finished a few pages, stop and share your work with an adult who cares about you. You will discover that you feel better after you have talked about your feelings and let others know what you need. I hope you will decide to share your book with everyone in your stepfamily. Feelings can be shared, problems can be solved and living together can be more fun.

My family has changed. This is a picture of my first family and the place we lived...

Memories are O.K. They build our future life.

We had happy times...   and not-so-happy times...

My first family ended because...

2.

For awhile, my parent wasn't married. We had...
<u>happy</u> times   and <u>not-so-happy</u> times

Change is part of life.

3.

Marriage brought happiness to my parent, but brought change into my life! (mark ✓ if there are a few changes.) (or ✓✓✓ if there are many changes.)

Home ____ family ____ school ____ church ____

Parent I live with ____ rules ____ allowance ____

Time together ____ time alone ____ friends ____

Food ____ money ____ fights ____ feelings ____

Other changes _____

The most difficult change for me is...

Some children have <u>two</u> places to live...
(Draw them if you do.)

Change brings many feelings.

This is a picture of me and my new stepfamily.

6. Stepfamilies have different beginnings. Different is O.K.

Stepfamilies may mean <u>more</u> parents, grandparents, siblings, aunts, uncles, cousins, neighbors and friends.

(Add names below circles. Color line <u>blue</u> if person has died. Draw faces and hair. Add red □ for each cousin, green ○ for each aunt and uncle and purple △ for new friends

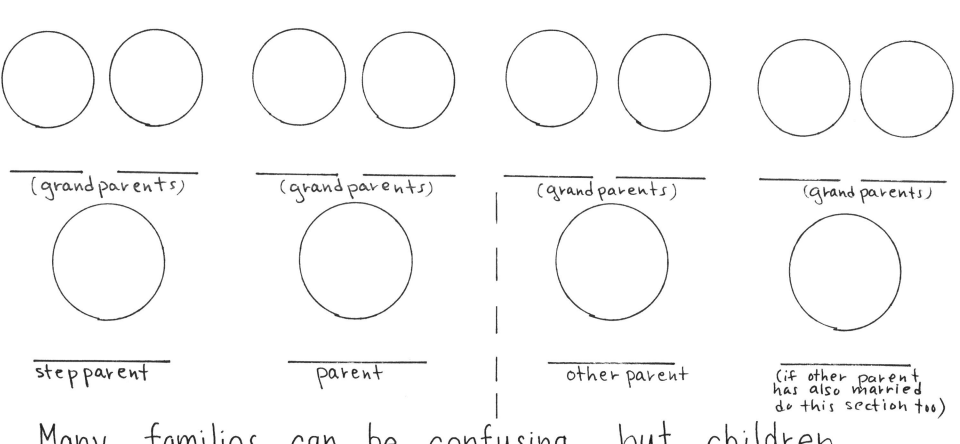

(grandparents)   (grandparents)   (grandparents)   (grandparents)

stepparent   parent   other parent   (if other parent has also married do this section too)

Many families can be confusing... but children can learn something good from each adult.

7.

Instant families can not expect <u>instant</u> love !
There will be problems... (draw some problems in your family)

8. Caring and trust will come in time.

Children and stepparents don't have to love each other... but they do need to respect each other.
(Put a ★ before each sentence you think is true and X if not true.)

1. Living with people means sharing time, people, things and space.

2. It is better for children when parents are happy.

3. Stepparents are wicked and mean to children.

4. Stepparents can become trusted friends with good advice when needed.

5. Step-sibs have different interests and abilities and cannot become good friends.

6. If stepparents have a baby, it is called a half-sib, but that doesn't mean half-as-good! It just means they have one same-parent instead of two.

7. Everyone must love everyone in a family.

8. Enjoying or loving a stepparent takes love away from a birth parent.

9. Stepfamilies have to learn to live with change.

9.

Change is a natural part of life. Things change... people change... families change. (draw a picture of any kind of change)

Families change when people are born or die, move in or out, get married or divorced.

Before stepfamilies come together, first families come apart bringing feelings of <u>loss and grief.</u>

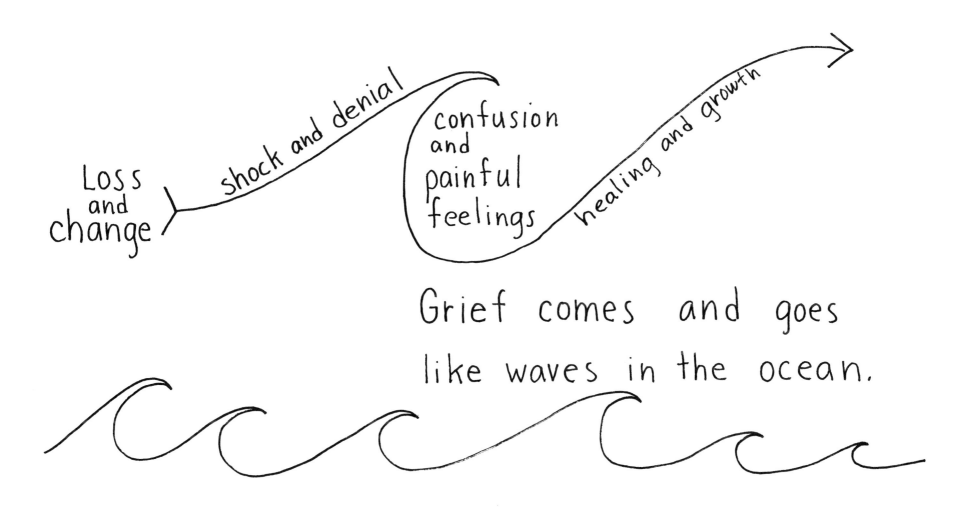

Loss and change

shock and denial

confusion and painful feelings

healing and growth

Grief comes and goes like waves in the ocean.

Children need to feel the feelings of loss before they can accept and welcome a new family.

When I was told my parent was going to get married, I...
(Draw what you felt and did.)

12. Feelings affect the way we act.

Feelings often show on faces... (Draw some feeling faces.)

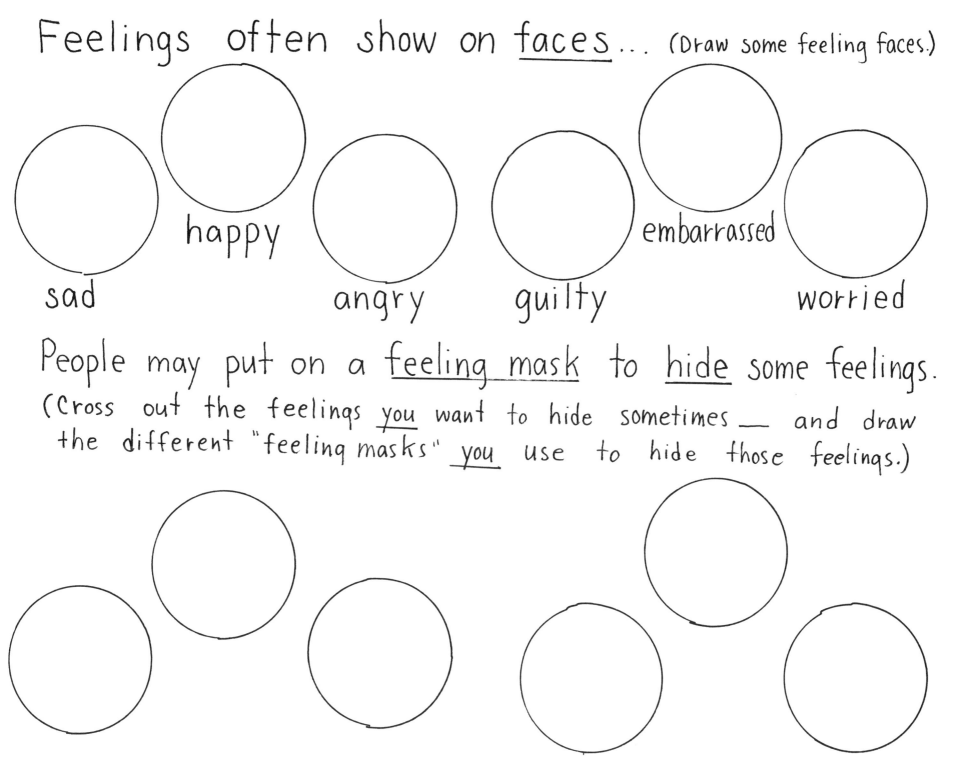

sad   happy   angry   guilty   embarrassed   worried

People may put on a <u>feeling mask</u> to <u>hide</u> some feelings.
(Cross out the feelings <u>you</u> want to hide sometimes ___ and draw the different "feeling masks" <u>you</u> use to hide those feelings.)

Feelings are something you feel in our body...
Where do you feel yours?

Close your eyes and
think about feeling times
and color the places you
feel your feelings with:

blue — sad
black — afraid
red — angry
green — jealous
orange — nervous
brown — guilty
yellow — happy

Feelings are all O.K.
If you keep your
feelings stuffed
inside too long,
they can cause
aches and pains.
Do you get aches
and pains in the
places you keep
feelings inside?

Exercise, sports, play, music, art, writing and
talking are all good ways to let feelings out.

14.

Check the feelings you feel <u>sometimes</u> with ✓ or <u>✓✓✓</u> if <u>often</u>. (underline any words you don't understand.)

helpless	nervous	smart
brave	sad	disloyal
lonely	unloved	disgusted
confused	ignored	jealous
proud	angry	shamed
loved	afraid	embarrassed
cheated	unsafe	frustrated
miserable	bored	disappointed
furious	special	guilty
stupid	happy	worried

15.

Children in stepfamilies have special feelings.

(Read and ★ those you sometimes feel.)

Some children:

1. Feel embarrassed about telling friends about marriage.
2. Feel jealous of the time parent spends with new spouse.
3. Feel angry about life changes because they didn't cause the death or divorce... and didn't choose new stepparent.
4. Resent too many people telling them what to do.
5. Feel caught in the middle and helpless.
6. Feel sad that stepparent doesn't seem to like them as much as his/her birth children.
7. Feel resentful because they don't think they are being treated fairly.
8. Worry that this marriage might end too.
9. Wish this marriage would end.
10. Feel happy because their parent is happy.

16.

There may be problems sharing space or time together. (Draw what is hardest for you.)

Everyone can try to be fair and learn how to cooperate.

17.

Different families have different <u>rules</u> and <u>discipline.</u>
(list some that are different now)

Churches, schools, playgrounds and friends have
18. different rules too.

Some things may not seem fair... (write or draw some)

Chores   Rules

Chores and rules must be different for different ages. Problems must be talked about.

19.

I get angry when...

It is O.K. to feel angry but it is not O.K. to
20. hurt people or things!

You can learn to let anger out in ways that will not hurt people or things.   O.K. ways are:

1. Saying "I am angry because..."
2. Punching a pillow or punching ball.
3. Yelling into a pillow or in the shower.
4. Stomping your feet or clapping your hands.
5. Write an angry letter and tear it up.
6. Writing in your journal.
7. Scribble on an old newspaper using alot of color and feeling. Scrunch it into a ball to toss at a blank wall.
8. Walk or run fast.

You are responsible for your behavior!

There is something I wish could be different...

All problems can not be fixed, but reactions to them
22. can be changed.

Sometimes I don't feel loved... (draw or write about it)

There are many kinds of love. Loving a spouse, child, parent or friend is different and special. Love never runs out.

23.

Sometimes I feel jealous because my parent is with my stepparent instead of me... (Draw those times.)

Everyone needs some special time. Adults need time together. A child can't replace a missing parent.

I can have fun just being a child again! (Draw
yourself having fun.)

My parent has another adult to share
parenting and adult worries.   25.

I have many people who care about me. (list name and put the number in the circle. ★ those you can talk to about problems.)

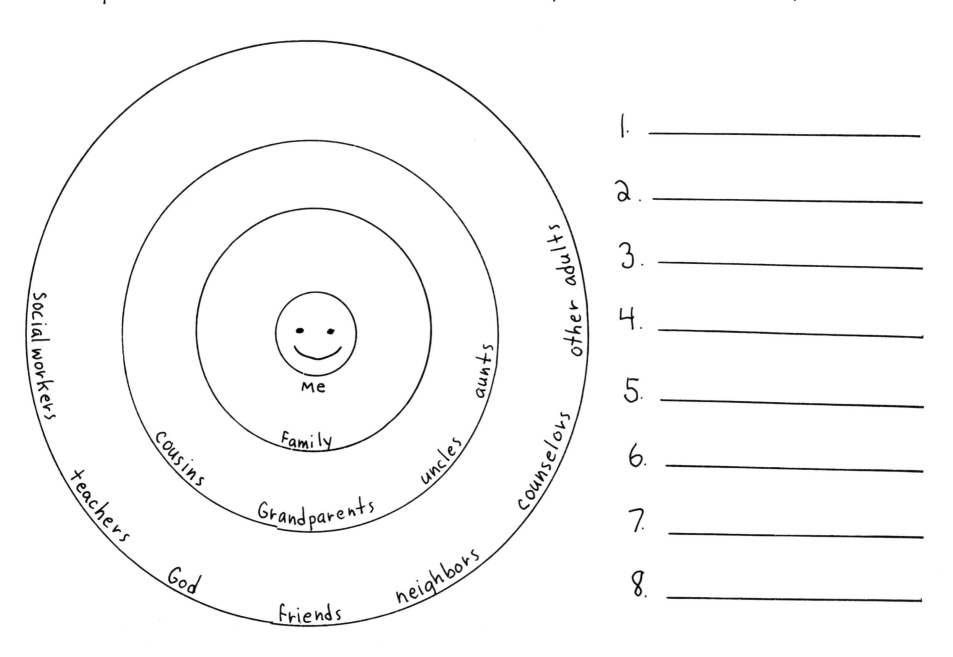

1. _____

2. _____

3. _____

4. _____

5. _____

6. _____

7. _____

8. _____

Sometimes I feel guilty ...

Guilt can be <u>real</u> or <u>imagined</u>. It is very important to talk to someone about it.

27.

Some things can be changed	Other things can not be changed

28. It is important to know the difference!

I try to treat others as I want to be treated.

A family is a group of people who live together.
They need to respect and help each other.

29.

There is something good about each person in my family. (write each name and draw or write what is good about them.)

30. "Put-ups" are better than "put-downs".

My birth parents will always be special to me

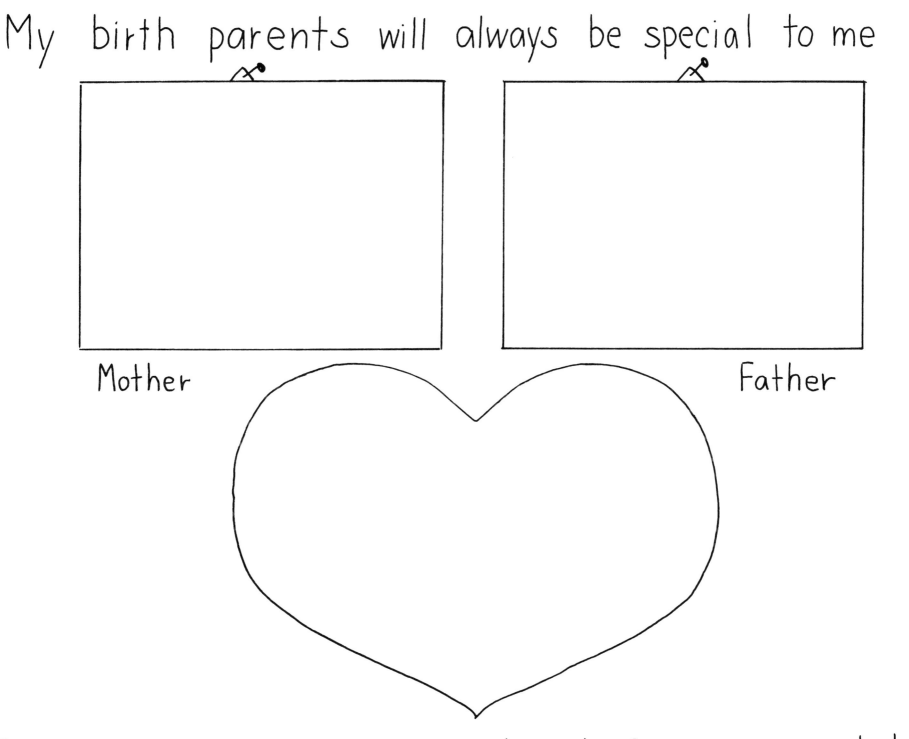

Mother

Father

But there is room in my heart for many people! 31.

My stepfamily can have fun together. (Draw something you would like to do with them.)

32. We will build good memories together.

The Drawing Out Feelings Series

This new series designed by Marge Heegaard provides parents and professionals with an organized approach to helping children ages 6-12 cope with feelings resulting from family loss and change.

Designed to be used in an adult/child setting, these workbooks provide age-appropriate educational concepts and questions to help children identify and accept their feelings. Children are given the opportunity to work out their emotions during difficult times while learning to recognize acceptable behavior, and conflicts can be resolved and self-esteem increased while the coping skills for loss and change are being developed.

All four titles are formatted so that children can easily illustrate their answers to the important questions in the text.

When Something Terrible Happens

A workbook to help children deal with their feelings about traumatic events.

Empowers children to explore feelings, and reduces nightmares and post-traumatic stress symptoms. "This healing book...combines story, pictures, information, and art therapy in a way that appeals to children." —Stephanie Frogge, Director of Victim Outreach, M.A.D.D.

Ages 6-12, 36 pp, 11x8 1/2", $6.95
trade paperback, ISBN 0-9620502-3-7

When Mom and Dad Separate

A workbook to help children deal with their feelings about separation/divorce.

This bestselling workbook helps youngsters discuss the basic concepts of marriage and divorce, allowing them to work through all the powerful and confusing feelings resulting from their parents' decision to separate.

Ages 6-12, 36 pp, 11x8 1/2", $6.95
trade paperback, ISBN 0-9620502-2-9

When Someone Has a Very Serious Illness

A workbook to help children deal with their feelings about serious illness.

An excellent resource for helping children learn the basic concepts of illness and various age-appropriate ways of coping with someone else's illness. "...offers children a positive tool for coping with those many changes." —Christine Ternand, M.D., Pediatrician

Ages 6-12, 41 pp, 11 x 8 1/2", $6.95
trade paperback, ISBN 0-9620502-4-5

When Someone Very Special Dies
Children Can Learn to Cope with Grief

A workbook to help children deal with their feelings about death.

Here is a practical format for allowing children to understand the concept of death and develop coping skills for life. Children, with adult supervision, are invited to illustrate and personalize their loss through art. This workbook encourages the child to identify support systems and personal strengths. "I especially appreciate the design of this book...the child becomes an active participant in pictorially and verbally doing something about [their loss]." —Dean J. Hempel, M.D., Child Psychiatrist

Ages 6-12
36 pp, 11 x 8 1/2", $6.95
trade paperback
ISBN 0-9620502-0-2

When a Family Is In Trouble
Children Can Cope With Grief From Drug and Alcohol Addictions

A workbook to help children through the trauma of a parent's chemical dependency problem.

This helpful workbook provides basic information about addictions and encourages healthy coping skills. Children express personal trauma and feelings more easily in pictures than in words, and the pages of this title are perfect to "draw out" those feelings and hurts. There is plenty of room for a child's artwork.

Ages 6-12
36 pp, 11 x 8 1/2", $6.95
trade paperback
ISBN 0-9620502-7-X

When a Parent Marries Again

A workbook to help children deal with their feelings about stepfamilies.

This book helps kids sort through unrealistic expectations, different values, divided loyalties, and family histories. It helps reduce the fear and stress surrounding remarriage and promotes greater family unity.

Ages 6-12, 36 pp, 11 x 8 1/2", $6.95
trade paperback, ISBN 0-9620502-6-1

Facilitator Guide For
DRAWING OUT FEELINGS

for
When Someone Very Special Dies
When Something Terrible Happens
When Someone Has a Very Serious Illness
When Mom and Dad Separate

Structure and suggestions for helping children, individually or in groups, cope with feelings from family change. Includes directions for six organized sessions for each of the four workbooks.
99 pp. 8 1/4 x 11 ISBN 0-9620502-5-3
$20.00

MARGE EATON HEEGAARD, MA, ATR, LICSW

Grades 3-6
64 pages $15.95

Stories about young people's grief and facts about death.

Coping with
Death & Grief

SEND THIS INFORMATION TO ORDER

SHIPPING CHARGES
up to 19.99 $2.50 * 20.00-44.99 $3.50 * 45.00-74.99 $4.50 * over 75.00 $5.50

___ Copies COPING WITH DEATH AND GRIEF ($15.95)
___ Copies DRAWING OUT FEELINGS GUIDE ($20.00)
___ Copies WHEN SOMEONE VERY SPECIAL DIES *
___ Copies WHEN SOMEONE HAS A VERY SERIOUS ILLNESS *
___ Copies WHEN SOMETHING TERRIBLE HAPPENS *
___ Copies WHEN MOM AND DAD SEPARATE *
___ Copies WHEN A PARENT MARRIES AGAIN *
___ Copies WHEN A FAMILY IS IN TROUBLE *

* at the following prices: *quantity discounts*

order amount	each cost	shipping
1-11	$ 6.95	$ 2.50
12-24	$ 4.50	$ 4.25
25-79	$ 4.00	$ 7.25
80-(same)	$ 3.50	$10.50

FOR FOREIGN ORDERS: PAYMENT IN USA FUNDS ONLY.
DOUBLE SHIPPING CHARGES.
Make check payable and send to: Total order _____
WOODLAND PRESS   MN. res. 6.5% _____
99 Woodland Circle   Handling _____
Minneapolis, MN. 55424   TOTAL COST _____
(612) 926-2665

NAME _____

ORGANIZATION _____

ADDRESS _____

_____

_____

TELEPHONE (_____) _____